The Philosophy of Self-Knowledge

By
Franz Hartmann

Copyright © 2022 Lamp of Trismegistus. All rights reserved. No part of this publication may be reproduced or transmitted in any form or by any means, electronic or mechanical, including photocopying, recording, or by any information storage and retrieval system, without permission in writing from Lamp of Trismegistus. Reviewers may quote brief passages.

ISBN: 978-1-63118-613-4

Esoteric Classics

Other Books in this Series and Related Titles

Aurora of the Philosophers by Paracelsus (978-1-63118-507-6)

Rosicrucian Rules, Secret Signs, Codes and Symbols by various (978-1-63118-488-8)

On the Philadelphian Gold by Philochrysus & Philadelphus (978-1-63118-511-3)

Paracelsus, the Four Elements and Their Spirits by M P Hall (978-1-63118-400-0)

The Stone of the Philosophers by A E Waite (978-1-63118-509-0)

Clairvoyance and Psychic Abilities by A Besant &c (978-1-63118-403-1)

The Rosicrucian Chemical Marriage by Christian Rosenkreuz (978-1-63118-458-1)

The Alchemical Catechism of Paracelsus by Paracelsus (978-1-63118-513-7)

Alchemy in the Nineteenth Century by Helena P. Blavatsky (978-1-63118-446-8)

Rosicrucians and Speculative Masonry in the Seventeenth Century (978-1-63118-489-5)

Qabbalistic Teachings and the Tree of Life by M P Hall (978-1-63118-482-6)

The Sepher Yetzirah and the Qabalah by M P Hall (978-1-63118-481-9)

The Devil in Love by Jacques Cazotte (978–1–63118–499–4)

Fortune-Telling with Dice by Astra Cielo (978-1-63118-466-6)

History, Analysis and Secret Tradition of the Tarot by Hall &c (978-1-63118-445-1)

Crystal Vision Through Crystal Gazing by Frater Achad (978-1-63118-455-0)

The Golden Verses of Pythagoras: Five Translations (978-1-63118-479-6)

Arcane Formulas or Mental Alchemy by W W Atkinson (978-1-63118-459-8)

The Machinery of the Mind by Dion Fortune (978-1-63118-451-2)

The A E Waite Reader: A Selection of Occult Essays (978-1-63118-515-1)

The Leadbeater Reader: A Selection of Occult Essays (978-1-63118-483-3)

Audio versions are also available on Audible, Amazon and Apple

Other Books in this Series and Related Titles

The Secrets of John Ernst Worrell Keely by Moore (978-1-63118-612-7)

Occult Symbolism of the Sun and Moon, the Goddess Isis and thee Solar Deities by Manly P Hall (978–1–63118–611–0)

Practical Theosophy by Annie Besant (978–1–63118–610–3)

The Human Body in Symbolism by Manly P Hall (978–1–63118–609–7)

Theosophical Basics by William Q Judge (978–1–63118–608–0)

The Hebrew Talisman by Richard Harte (978–1–63118–607–3)

Early Masonic Symbolism by Manly P Hall (978–1–63118–606–6)

Nature Spirits and Elementals by Louise Off (978-1-63118-605-9)

Swedenborg Bifrons by H P Blavatsky (978-1-63118-604-2)

Practical Use of Psychic Powers by C W Leadbeater (978-1-63118-603-5)

Using White & Black Magic by C W Leadbeater (978-1-63118-602-8)

Jesus, the Last Great Initiate by Edouard Schure (978-1-63118-599-1)

Mysterious Wonders of Antiquity by Manly P Hall (978-1-63118-598-4)

Ancient Mysteries and Secret Societies by Manly P Hall (978–1–63118–597–7)

The Zodiac and Its Signs by Manly P Hall (978–1–63118–596–0)

Life and Teachings of Hermes Trismegistus by Manly P Hall (978–1–63118–595–3)

The Secrets of Doctor Taverner by Dion Fortune (978–1–63118–594–6)

Vegetarianism, Theosophy & Occultism by Leadbeater &c (978–1–63118–593–9)

Applied Theosophy by Henry S Olcott (978–1–63118–592–2)

Higher Consciousness by C W Leadbeater (978–1–63118–591–5)

Theories About Reincarnation and Spirits by H P Blavatsky (978–1–63118–590–8)

Audio versions are also available on Audible, Amazon and Apple

Table of Contents

Introduction...7

*The Philosophy of Self Knowledge
Or
The Mystery of the Three Words
Revealing Itself in Man*

Preface...9

The Philosophy...11

Oracles
from Thomas Taylor...36

INTRODUCTION

The word "esoteric" can be difficult to define. Esotericism in general can be seen less as a system of beliefs and more as a category, which encompasses numerous, different systems of beliefs. It's a bit of juxtaposition, since the word "esoteric" indicates something that few people know about, while the term itself broadly covers numerous philosophies, practices, areas of study and belief systems.

In a greater sense, Esotericism acts as a storehouse for secret knowledge, which is often considered ancient (by *tradition, if not by fact*), passed down from generation to generation, in private. At various times in history, simply possessing the knowledge of some of these subjects, was considered illegal and a jailable offence, if discovered. This usually included such general topics as Alchemy, Pharmacology, Qabalah, Hermeticism, Occultism, Ceremonial Magic, Astrology, Divination, Rosicrucianism and so on. Collectively, these areas of study were often referred to as the esoteric sciences.

Sometimes, the outer garment of a subject isn't esoteric, while what is hidden beneath it, is. As an example, Freemasonry isn't necessarily esoteric by nature (at *least not anymore*), but certain signs, passwords and handshakes given to the candidate during their initiation, are in fact, esoteric, in the sense that they are hidden from the general public.

Today, in the twenty-first century, such topics are readily available at bookstores across the country, and numerous main-steam publishers offer beginners guides and coffee-table volumes on many of these subjects, intended for mass appeal. Books like *"The Secret"* have turned previously arcane topics into household knowledge. All that being the case, however, it isn't to say that there still aren't buried secrets to uncover, ancient wisdom being ignored and forgotten mysteries to be explored. In fact, it is often that we are only able to further our own studies by standing on the shoulders of these disappearing giants.

Lamp of Trismegistus is doing its part to help preserve humanity's esoteric history by making some of these classics available to those students who are seeking to unearth the knowledge of these ancient colossi.

So, be sure to check other titles from our *Esoteric Classics* series, as well as our *Occult Fiction, Theosophical Classics, Foundations of Freemasonry Series, Supernatural Fiction, Paranormal Research Series, Studies in Buddhism* and our *Christian Apocrypha Series.* You can also download the audio versions of most of these titles from Amazon, Apple or Audible, for learning on the go.

THE PHILOSOPHY OF SELF-KNOWLEDGE
or
The Mystery of the Three Worlds Revealing Itself in Man

by Franz Hartmann

"The true state of being begins only with the attainment of the knowledge of the true Self."

PREFACE

THE object of the following pages is to aid those who are in search of the truth in realizing that there is no other real knowledge, except the knowledge of the reality in one's own soul. The reality in man is the truth, and although truth is eternal and independent of the recognition of men, nevertheless it is nothing to men if they do not realize its existence. He who refuses to seek for the light within himself will not find the true light anywhere in externals, and will continue to dwell in his darkness. He who finds truth within himself will also recognize the spirit of truth throughout all nature; for it is the spirit of truth in him who recognizes itself in everything.

There are many ways of drawing a picture of nature, and each of them may be true. Nature is only one, but it represents itself to man in various aspects. While in the tropical south nature is adorned with a luxurious vegetation, in the cold regions of the polar seas it is clothed in snow and ice, and to the inhabitant of either zone the sights of the other appear unfamiliar and perhaps improbable. Thus there are many ways of describing the way in which the truth manifests itself in the heart and mind and the actions of man; and whether we describe it in intricate Sanskrit terms or in the more familiar language of the West, it will lead to the same result, provided that we do not misinterpret the meaning of the words used in the description. We claim no dogmatic belief and no authority whatever except such as comes from the self-perception of truth in ourselves, and we merely ask those who are inclined to doubt the truth of the statements contained in these pages to appeal for its confirmation to the power of truth within themselves, and to remember that not the imagination of the speculative brain, but only the spirit and light of God in the heart and mind, can penetrate into the mysteries of divine being.

THE PHIILOSOPHY

He who knows others is clever; he who knows himself is illumined.

-oOo-

The unknown exercises a great fascination over the mind of man. We are told that for ages, man, in an ethereal or spiritual state, rested in his paradisiacal surroundings in blissful ignorance of evil and suffering, until, when he ate of the fruit of self-will, which he plucked from the tree of life, he descended into a more material state, a lower nature became developed in him, and he became entangled in the wilderness of delusions, losing sight of the light of divine truth. This allegory, far from being restricted to illustrate merely a historical occurrence having taken place in the forgotten past, states what may be seen to take place every day; for now, as in times of old, the soul of man is attracted to what he loves, and therefore the seeking for the knowledge of good is good, and the seeking for the knowledge of evil is attended by evil results. Even this day and in millions of human beings, "*Eve*" (the will) stretches forth her hand to pluck the fruit from the tree of knowledge of that which is pleasing to the senses, but nevertheless false and deceptive, and for ever the "*Adam*" (the intelligence) in man is willing to taste. The eyes of the king of the world, whose name is sensuality, for ever seek within the depths of gross matter for the treasures by which selfish desires may be gratified and passing comforts obtained; for that king is an animal and has no wings for rising upwards towards the realm of freedom. He keeps imprisoned within his grossly material nature that part of man's soul which is of a higher origin. Digging the earth in search of the gold of wisdom, he rejoices when he finds only worms. Fortunate is he in whom during the struggle for terrestrial existence the celestial part of his nature does not become unconscious of its own true nature and majesty, remembering that it is a child of the kingdom of light.

The tendencies for good and for evil, and also the power of receiving external impressions, are dwelling in man's own little world, and the good and evil and the attractions of external nature, by which he is surrounded, act powerfully upon the corresponding elements in his constitution. From the action of good and evil tendencies and desires in him which are the results of his past experiences, results the duality of his will, in which either good or evil inclinations may preponderate; while, by means of the impressions he receives from external nature he receives a continual influx, of food for thought, which he may use according to the capacity of his understanding, either for aiding him in realizing the truth, or for the purpose of feeding his fancies.

The desire of obtaining real knowledge of a thing is inseparable from a desire for realizing its qualities. To realize qualities is to possess them. To thoroughly love is to become. To love to know the high is to become exalted; to earnestly desire the low is to become degraded. Love and desire are qualities of the will, and the will is "the heart" of man. "Wherever one's treasure is, there is one's heart"; "where the carrion lies, there will the eagles assemble." The continued desire for unreasonable things leads to the loss of reason; the love of divine truth opens the portals of wisdom. To seek to know a thing, not merely superficially, or for the love of gratifying one's curiosity, but for the love of the thing itself, is to approach its essence and to enter into its sphere. Therefore the revelation of a heretofore unknown great truth fills the soul with delight; while the realization of a heretofore unknown evil causes it to be pervaded by terror, evil being perverted good and therefore a falsehood. To realize a new truth means the opening of the eyes to a new light of the understanding; it means the initiation into a new state of existence, the awakening of a new life.

Such a state of self-knowledge is not attained merely by believing in some new information received from somebody, nor by the accepting of some new opinion which seems more plausible than the ones that were held before. True enough, the soul may rejoice in believing of having found a new truth by discovering a new theory; but such joy is not the same and not so convincing as that which arises from the self-recognition of divine truth in oneself, and it is merely caused by the gratification of some illusive desire, forming a part of oneself, but not by the realization of one's own true self. It is as different from realizing the truth, as the holding to a favourite opinion about the nature of a thing differs from seeing and feeling and entering into the state of that thing, and being that thing itself. *To realize is to be. To truly know is to become.* The attainment of real knowledge involves an internal transformation of one's own being; it is not a mere "science", but an entering into truth.

Thus, for instance, if we were to believe that the stars in the sky were merely lights, nailed to a solid vault constituting the firmament, and it were then demonstrated to us by logical inferences that this theory cannot be true, and that these stars are inhabited worlds, or suns around which revolve inhabited planets, such an enlargement of our conception would surely fill us with joy as soon as we would give room in our mind to this new theory, because we behold a glimpse of a new truth; but nevertheless it would still be merely a theory, and not approach that realization of truth which would result if we could leave our terrestrial form upon the earth and visit ourselves the planets in space and become ourselves their temporary inhabitants. If we had passed through such an experience, we might then well afford to laugh at any theory to the contrary which a mere "scientist" might advance and which would be opposed to our self-

13

knowledge. We would be in regard to him in the same position as he would be in regard to an Australian savage who were to dispute with him the possibility of making railways and telegraphs.

What is self-knowledge? The dictionary informs us that it is the knowledge of one's own real character. But my character is myself, my own substance. My character is that which characterizes my own state of existence; I cannot actually realize anything that is foreign to me. Real knowledge is the realization of one's own real state of being. I cannot realize anything unless I have the power to do so. It will therefore be correct to say: "Self-knowledge is the power by which a being truly realizes its own state of existence. Real self-knowledge is the power by which the eternal reality realizes its own real existence in man."

There can be only one true self-knowledge, namely, the self-realization of truth; for that which is false is not true, and if there is no truth in it there can be no power in it for recognizing that truth which does not exist. In every being in which there is a spark of truth, there is also a spark of the power for attaining self-knowledge; but this spark only becomes a power when it begins to act. A power is a principle, and "principle" means a *beginning* capable of growth. That which does not begin to exist has no existence in him in whom it does not grow and enter in power. True self-knowledge is the manifestation of the power of truth to reveal itself in man. Man cannot by his own power reveal the truth to himself; he cannot himself create a power which he does not possess; he is not a "truth maker", and that which is false in him can have no self-perception of truth. The darkness in him can never attain the realization of its being the light, because it is not the light; it is only the light of truth in him, eternal, uncreated and self-existent, that can realize its own existence in him, and thus lead him up to a recognition of truth by entering himself into its light, in which there is no limitation of self; for truth is universal and only one.

There can be no other real knowledge than the realization of the real within oneself. This is so self-evident, that it would hardly be worth the while to dwell upon this fact, if it were not for the circumstance that while this truth is universally admitted in theory, it is also universally disregarded in practice, because it is generally only believed in by the intellect, and not truly realized by the understanding. Thus merely negative science is often mistaken for positive knowledge, and a mind full of adopted opinions forms that treasure of imaginary self-knowledge of which many learned persons are proud. There are many who believe that they know almost everything that can possibly be known, while they are forced to admit that they do not know their own self; but if any one does not know the true self in him, how can he consistently affirm that this self, which he does not know, knows anything whatever? If the "self" which in him seems to know, is false, then surely its so-called knowledge is equally false and illusive, and does not belong to himself. If the presence and power of the true, the only real and divine self in man is not recognized by man, or to express it in other words, if he wilfully refuses to recognize the power of the spirit of God in him, which is the light and the truth, and his Christ and Redeemer, how then could the truth realize its existence in him, and he enter into its light?

Every being constitutes a certain state of the one universal consciousness, and it cannot be self-conscious of anything higher than that which it is itself. An animal can have no higher self-consciousness than that which belongs to an animal; the lower mind in man can have no self-consciousness of being the higher mind. A man may fancy himself to be a god, but he can have no real knowledge of God unless he enters into the divine state, when God will know himself in him, a state which is conditioned by his giving up the delusion of what is commonly called "self". There is no power, no principle, no being, that can rise above its own level, its own state of existence, except by being changed into something higher, by the power of the highest becoming active within its own constitution. Mortal man, being not immortal, cannot save himself or confer immortality upon himself; he can only be saved by the power of his own true real self, which is already immortal and which will render him so as soon as he is ready to realize his oneness with the immortal being in him.

Man has always been a conundrum unto himself, and will remain misunderstood as long as he refuses to recognize the truth hidden within himself, and mistakes his ever-changing personality for his real self. There are two natures in man. One is the product of the manifestation of truth in him, it is a child of light and easily understood by itself, for its knowledge does not consist in vagaries or in a collection of opinions; it is itself a manifestation of truth, and therefore it knows the truth in itself. The other nature is a product of darkness and misconception, it will remain forever incomprehensible, because it continually changes, even while we are investigating its character; it is one compound today and will be another compound tomorrow. The real self is filled with joy and tranquillity; in the illusive "self" rules discontent, confusion and unrest, it does not enjoy, peace and silence, tranquillity is a torment to it.

That which at the present stage of evolution the majority of men and women fancy to be their "self" is not their true real self. The latter is a manifestation of the true light; the former its changeful shadow by which the eternal image of God in man has become turned into a caricature. No one can really know what "man" really is unless he has himself begun to be truly and in reality *a man*.

Oh, the joy and freedom, the sublime peace and serene tranquillity that enter the heart of man if by the fulfilment of some high duty he becomes self-conscious even for one short moment of what it means to be truly *a man*, and seeing himself reflecting the true image of his own inner God. When this truth is revealed to him — not by the reading of books, nor by any information received from external sources — but by the power of his own true manhood manifesting itself within his own constitution and penetrating even the physical form, then during such a moment will he be in possession of a ray of the light of real knowledge. little will he care during such a moment what classification of his principles is accepted by science, or what are the views of the philosophers regarding the constitution of man. He knows himself to be, for no other reason except that his God in him recognizes himself in him, and this is sufficient for his purpose — which is to enjoy the presence of divine truth. All other knowledge, such as does not consist in the self-realization of truth in oneself, does not constitute real knowledge, and can have no other ultimate object than by destroying the misconceptions of truth which exist in the mind, to make the mind receptive for the light of eternal truth, in which alone rests the power of the true understanding. There is no other way to real knowledge except the self-recognition of truth.

Man's constitution may be compared with a harp of many strings, some representing a high and others a lower scale. Some give discordant, others concordant sounds. If a man identifies himself with one of these strings constituting his harp, he will be harmonious or inharmonious according to its quality. He will be played upon by the forces of nature, but he will not be the master of the instrument. Only he who rises by the power of the divine will in him beyond the realm of illusion, he in whom the truth realizes its own eternal reality, will be removed beyond pleasure and pain, and may use his own instrument in praise of divine wisdom.

Truly there is nothing which a man can really call permanently his own, except that power which is permanent in him, and which constitutes his real self — the light of eternal truth in him. Man's body belongs to material nature, his animal emotions to the animal soul of the world; his intellectual acquisitions are the result of play of the intellectual powers in him. Only his spirit belongs to God, and the self-consciousness of the divine spirit within his soul is all that really constitutes his own individuality. Once attained, this spiritual self-consciousness of the truth, the real in man, constitutes the inextinguishable light which will illuminate his path in the darkness during his terrestrial life and in eternity. This world with its illusions does not belong to that which is real in man. It is merely a school of learning, and the knowledge to be acquired therein is the realization of its impermanency and worthlessness. Man in this mundane existence is like a pilgrim in a foreign land, where he is for a while housed and fed, but not permitted to remain. Physical life is for him like a book, lent to him for the purpose of learning the follies described therein; it is not his own permanent property, but has to be returned to the library when the time of his lesson is ended. All that man really can possess and keep is his own inner spiritual life, which is non-existent for him as long as he is not conscious of its possession. Therefore, the divine knowledge of self is the highest good; it is a creative power which eternally manifests itself in creating worlds, for it is the self-conscious will of God in man, beholding itself in its own light of divine wisdom. Therefore, the greatest advice that was ever given by any sage is: "*Man, know thyself*".

What does self-knowledge embrace? The answer to this is plain. It can embrace neither more nor less but the qualities of one's self. The self-knowledge of the illusive self is an illusion, the self-knowledge of the real self is the realization of truth. Truth is the only universal reality, and therefore true self-knowledge embraces the all. Nothing can therefore exist outside of the self-knowledge of God in the divine man, and this fact becomes still more evident if we consider that all that exists in its original state is a manifestation of divine wisdom.

Let not the reader refuse to recognize this truth within his own soul because his limited intellect is unable to grasp it. That which is finite cannot comprehend the infinite; the creature cannot rise above the creator; the form is not greater than the spirit of which it is a symbol and external expression. The mortal intellect cannot have self-knowledge of its own divinity, because it is not divine; divine wisdom does not belong to a man without truth, it belongs only to God, and he who wants to acquire it must die in regard to his own illusive self with all its possessions, and not become merely "godlike", but God himself, by having his so-called "self" absorbed in and transmuted in the power of God in him. *To know* in spirit and in truth means *to be*. No one can know life unless he is living; to know what is consciousness one must be conscious; to know desire one must be in its possession; only the just can know the manifestation of justice; the true the manifestation of truth; the beautiful soul the manifestations of beauty; the harmonious harmony, etc. To know the essential nature of any spiritual power it is necessary to step out of the narrow limits of "self". That self, which is the product of darkness, must be abandoned and disappear if the light is to manifest itself to itself in man. Man can know nothing real about the attributes of his own divine powers, if not by means of the disappearance of his illusions these divine attributes attain self-knowledge in and through him.

Thus it appears to be plain that *each principle can have real knowledge only of its own self,* and of nothing else. Each can truly realize only its own reality, but not the reality of another. If man were formed only of one principle he could know only one thing, because only that one principle and none other could attain self-consciousness and self-knowledge in him. But the mind (*manas*) of man is a "mixed being"; in man all the three kingdoms — the realm of light (the truth), the realm of darkness (illusion), and the kingdom of external nature — are fully and completely contained, and each of these kingdoms is seeking to manifest itself in him. Therefore he is called the "lord of creation", because all the powers of heaven and hell and of physical nature are striving to assume form and become manifested in him. All these powers are striving in him for the attainment of life and self-consciousness; or, as *Angelus Silesius* expresses it: "All nature rushes to man, so that man may lead it to the knowledge of God", Man's mind may be compared to a mirror, in which all things may be reflected, be they good or evil or a mixture of both; but the images in his mind are not unsubstantial images like those in a looking-glass, they attain life and consciousness and substance in him; and as in a forest a tall tree springs from a tiny seed, fed by sunshine and water and air and drawing nutriment from the soil, so the seed of an emotion taking root in his soul may grow; an idea for good or for evil, forming itself into a thought, taking shape in the realm of his imagination, being fed by the power arising from the material body, being "watered" by his will and receiving life from the reflection of the light of the spirit within. Man's desires, thoughts and ideas form the plants that grow in the garden of his mind. The light of spirit within his heart causes them all to grow. If the seeds are evil the products will be noxious growths; if the seeds are good the results will be beautiful. Each product is a being, an entity in itself; be its existence of ever so short a duration, each may according to the action of the will of man grow and become manifested in him, and even become his master and make him its slave — for experience teaches that there are many persons whose minds are so full of opinions, speculations, chimeras, phantasms and morbid desires, that there is no room in them for the manifestation of the light of divine wisdom.

Everybody knows that what a man actually perceives of any external object, is not that object itself, but the impression he receives from it by means of his senses. Thus the lover is actually in love only with the image of the beloved which has assumed a form within his own mind, and he endows his own creation with his own desires and qualities; so that, as it often happens, his ideal conception of the beloved person does not at all correspond with the qualities of the original; and when he discovers the difference between the two there is an end to his love. Thus we may say that the image of the beloved ideal has become a conscious entity within his mind, and seeing its own qualities reflected in the beloved object, it loves itself in that object, until it finds out its mistake and sees that this object is not a true representation of its own qualities; for love is a principle, a unity, and can know nothing else but itself, love is always *self-love*, in every state of existence, and even the highest manifestation of love, divine and universal love, is the love of God in man, recognizing its own existence in everything in the universe.

As with love, so it is with every other power, or with the manifestation of a power as an image or form. Man is continually subjected to the action of powers that have become developed in him, and he is continually encompassed by his own creations, even if they are not all at all times present before his consciousness. As the clouds float in the atmosphere surrounding our planets, so the creations in the mind of man move above in his mental sphere. They are living and relatively substantial entities, drawing their life and consciousness from their creator. These "spirits" may be his guardian angels or his destroyers; they may lead him to the perception of truth or veil him in darkness.

If a person has possession of a well-developed idea, that idea forms a part of his nature and has also possession of him. The first sight of an entirely new and unknown thing, such as a steam-engine would be to a savage, produces no perceptible definite impression upon the mind; an idea has to take root in the mind and grow, so to say, into an organ of interior sense before it can attain self-consciousness therein and the mind know its nature. When this is accomplished, it will be as true to say "the idea works through the man", as it is to say "the man works through the idea". Thus in an experienced engineer the idea of the engine with which he works, has become an entity in his mind, which supervises the external original. The engineer does not need to have the image of the engine continually objectively before his mental vision. It is, so to say, the living idea of the engine existing in his mind, which supervises and attends to the objective engine through the instrumentality of the engineer, who may often be seen to attend to his work instinctively and without ratiocination. In the same way one of whom a certain passion has taken possession, will act according to the dictates of his passion, without elaborate mental reflection; and one in whom divine love, wisdom and truth have grown into power will instinctively act according to their dictates and as their instrument, without going to consult the views of his intellect, or considering his personal desires.

He who says: "I am good, I am virtuous, I am wise, I am beautiful", etc., is deluded; for he attributes to his illusion of self, qualities which that "self", being an illusion, cannot possess in reality, and of which it can at best express outward effects, in the same sense as a cloud, tinctured with crimson and gold by the setting sun, is not the light of the sun, but merely an object on which the light is manifesting its beauty. The conception of the personal self, far from being necessary for the attainment of wisdom, is in fact the greatest obstacle in its way. "*Persona*" means "mask"; our personal self is merely the mask in which in our impersonal self is forced to parade during its pilgrimage upon the earth, and when true self-knowledge is attained, the illusory character of the mask will be realized. Instead of seeking to be good and virtuous, etc. ourselves, we should seek to let goodness, virtue, truth, beauty, justice, etc. become manifested in us; and there is nothing to hinder the manifestation of these powers in us, except that very clinging to the personal limited self, which is to be overcome by the power of the higher understanding. The personal delusion of self can have no real knowledge of truth, because it is not true, but delusive; its very limitation and separateness prevents it from knowing that which is *one* and universal and infinite. But he who by entering into the kingdom of truth has outgrown the conceit of the narrow "self," and in whom the truth has grown into power may truly say, " */ am the truth* ! " for it is not "he" (his personality) speaking these words, but the truth itself having attained self-knowledge in him, speaking these words through his mouth, and being the truth, it cannot say anything else but what is true.

Truth is a nothing to us as long as we are nothing in regard to the truth. The reason why only few are recognizing the nature of truth in the world is because in the many divine truth has not yet become manifest, owing to their love for the illusion of "self". Only he in whom the truth has become manifest can recognize the nature of the one truth in the universe; for each principle can have real knowledge only of its own self. He who is full of falsehoods and entangled in lies, will never know the truth unless he rises above his delusion, even if the truth were placed before his eyes. He will not attain it neither by external observation nor by logical inferences, nor by means of philosophical speculations, mathematical calculations, information coming from accepted authorities, or any so-called "revelations" coming from any outside source whatever. All such things can only give him certain ideas and opinions of what the truth *appears to be*, but nothing less than the truth in him, having grown into power, can endow him with real knowledge of that which is true. The light of the true understanding is not manufactured by any man; it is like the sunshine; no man can make it shine, he can only step out of the darkness and open his eyes to receive it, and if there is any principle of light in himself, then will the light from without call forth his internal light, rouse his power of seeing into action, and he will see the light, and through the light in him recognize the light in the world.

If then we wish to attain real knowledge of eternal truth, and to truly know our own real self, we must keep our inner eye directed steadfastly upon the sunlight of truth in ourselves. The truth is the *one unity* — the reality; man without truth is a nought. If the noughts are put before the one they are of no value, but if the nought is put after the one it gives to the one ten times its value. Reasoning without reason is worthless; only if we stand upon the basis of reason can our reasoning be of some use. True learning is useful, but the acquisition of knowledge in which there is no foundation of truth is destructive. External science, if based upon perception of the appearance of truth, is not an impediment, but rather an aid in opening one's eyes to the attainment of self-knowledge; but a science based upon mere outward and delusive appearances leads away from the self-recognition of truth. Therefore M. de Molinos says: "Ordinarily it is seen that in the man who hath much scholastical and speculative knowledge divine wisdom doth not predominate; yet they make an admirable composition when they both meet together, The men of learning who by God's mercy have attained to this mystic science, are worthy of veneration and praise in religion." [M. de Molinos, "The Spiritual Guide".]

Everywhere resounds the cry: "Lo! here is the truth!" and "there is the truth!" but the truth is everywhere for him in whom it is a living power, and it is nowhere for him in whose soul it is not manifest. Everything in nature is a symbol expressing a truth, but we must have truth in ourselves if we wish to understand the meaning of the symbols. It is of little use to enter a church edifice for the purpose of offering selfish petitions. If we realize that we ourselves are temples of the living God, then will the meaning of the symbol represented by the external temple also be clear. If I know the light of the truth in my heart, I will without further explanation know the meaning of the light which burns in the sanctuary of the church edifice. Every symbol is true if it is representing a truth, but if the truth which it is to represent does not exist, then is the symbol a representation of nothing, a mere pretension, a lie.

Thus a man is a walking lie if in dress, external appearance, title or position he represents a character or power which he does not truly possess. A black coat does not make a spiritual guide, a diploma does not make a true physician, a man in the garb of a saint, in whom there is no sanctity manifest, is merely a man masquerading in the garb of a saint and nothing more. If personal man is to know God, God must become personified in him; if he wants to attain real knowledge of the devil, the devil must take form in him and render him a personal devil. If he wants to attain real knowledge of the essence of natural things he must be able to perceive in all of his internal senses the truth of such things by the power of truth in himself.

It has often been stated that man has been made in the image of God. This means that man in his purity is an undefiled expression of divine truth, but he cannot be or become again such an expression unless the truth in its purity becomes manifested in and through his own substance; the falsehoods finding expression in him are not manifestations of truth — they do not represent his true self. If it is stated that his personality his mask, is merely an illusion, this does not mean that this personality does not exist, but that the consciousness of that personality does not constitute the true self-consciousness of the real and inner man. This personality is a compound of many and ever-changing states of consciousness, the total of which produces a focus of illusory self-consciousness, in which we find our personal identity, but which is not our real self. Our real self is the self-consciousness of God in us, a self-consciousness which is attained only by few, while those who have not attained it live in an illusory state an illusory life. The so-called self-consciousness of the ordinary personality rests therefore in misconception and ignorance, that of the true self in the self-recognition of divine truth. The former is the compound result of the aggregate of many conscious and ever-changing powers in us; the latter is simple, permanent and pure, it is the self-consciousness of eternal truth in man.

The true self is infinite; the falsehood of personal identity is within narrow limits, and the more the mind is captured by this narrow conception, the narrower will it grow until insanity is the end. In the true self-consciousness of the divine man is freedom and rest, the misconceptions in man constituting his false *egos* are continually at war with each other, being engaged in the struggle for existence. Sometimes one and at other times another of these impermanent states of consciousness and will attain mastery in him over the rest, and as his mind becomes tinctured either with one or another, his personal identity changes, although his outward appearance remains on the whole the same, owing to the slow changes taking place in his physical body, on account of the grossness and inertia of its material constituents, but the true *master* in him, the truth, does not change; it is indestructible. The truth having become self-conscious in him, is his "*Christ*" his own saviour. It redeems him by bringing him from the darkness of ignorance and falsehood into the light of divine wisdom.

If this truth were truly realized (but it cannot be realized by anything less than the divine part in man) then would the world as it is at present indeed appear as a great insane asylum filled with elementals and animals in human forms, but with very little real humanity being manifested therein. It is, however, of little use to preach against the "illusions of life", while recognition is refused to the existence of truth, for that which is nothing cannot make itself into something. The object of existence cannot be, as certain philosophers put it, "the negation of the will to live," nor "a giving up of one's will", but an entering into a higher and everlasting life by arising out of the narrow grave of illusion of the so-called self-will into the will of the true self, by means of which the personal will enters into harmony and becomes one with the divine.

The unity and universality of the true nature in man, *i.e.,* the divine humanity in him, has been recognized by all great souls and true philosophers in all countries, irrespective of the systems of religion to which they held. It is the doctrine of the *Vedas* and of the *Bible*; it has been recognized by Christian saints and philosophers, and by the initiates of every nation. It forms the sum and substance of the teachings of Angelus Silesius, Michael de Molinos, Jacob Boehme, Paracelsus, and is taught throughout Christendom, although perhaps the majority of its modern professional teachers do not really know or believe it themselves. Even some so-called "infidels" have recognized its truth. Thus in Voltaire's cottage, near Geneva in Switzerland, there is an inscription composed by himself, saying: "*Mon esprit est partout, et mon coeur est ici*". (My spirit is everywhere, and my heart is here.) The true man is everywhere, but the desires that belong to that part of his nature which does not recognize itself as being one with the God of the universe, form the ties that bind him to the material plane. If soul and spirit were fully united in one, then would man be free in the realization of his freedom, *i.e.,* in the self-knowledge of divine and universal truth, and his outward form would become a true expression of the manifestation of truth. Then would the misconception of his separateness disappear, and he would recognize his true individuality, or to express it in other words, the aggregate of his false *egos* would no longer produce in him the illusion that they are his real self; but these false *egos* having disappeared, he would recognize himself to be a universal being, and his form a local manifestation and personification of truth.

The divine life in humanity is the tree, the colours which characterize our individuality are the branches; but the personalities of men and women are the leaves which drop away in autumn and grow again in the spring. Man's divine self-consciousness is a light which in no way differs from the light of divine self-consciousness in all others, for it comes in all from the same source; but while in some it shines bright, there are others in which it has only begun to become manifest, and there are many in whom it is in an entirely latent state, because they cling to the darkness. If the truth is permitted to manifest itself in the soul (the life), then will the soul become luminous and self-conscious in its light, and grow into power; and if this power were permitted to manifest itself in all parts of the body, then would the whole body become self-conscious and luminous in the light of the soul, such as is actually the case with the bodies of the Adepts. We are all "temples of God", and the holy spirit of God dwells in us, but we know it not, and because we do not know it, we do not keep our temple pure enough for God to be born and personified in us, and the spirit of God flows in and out without becoming substantial in us, and without taking up in us its permanent habitation.

There is no manifestation of spirit possible without a substantial organism of some kind, be it of physical, psychical or any other kind of matter; but the body is also the cause of the delusion of separateness, isolation and "self". Our true self is not our limited form; our form is only an instrument of its manifestation; a true symbol and expression if it expresses the truth, a caricature if it expresses falsehood. The true self of man is too great, too unlimited, to be wholly enclosed in a limited form. How insignificant is the terrestrial body of man if compared with the spirit that strives to become manifested in it. Even external nature preaches to mortal man his insignificance. If from the top of a high mountain we look down upon the valley below where we see human beings move about like tiny specks of matter, how little do they appear! Looked at from such a distance all of man's works appear insignificant. His houses and palaces and the railway train as it creeps over the plains appear like toys of children, and while it seems to him who stands upon the summit as if he were an inhabitant of the air, he is inclined to pity the beings that crawl upon the earth. Thus, if by the wings of the free will of the soul man is carried up into the kingdom of truth, how insignificant appear the illusions of life, to which so much importance is attributed. In the unlimited expansion of the soul how infinitely little appears that insignificant "self", around which, nevertheless, all of mortal man's earthly hopes and desires are centred, and to which he clings with so much tenacity, because he does not recognize the power which is its fountain and its creator.

We do not recognize the power of universal life, because it never represents itself to us in an objective state apart from its manifestation. We only know of its manifestation in some objective form, and thus we mistake the expression of life for life, and the form for the spirit; but the capacity of feeling the power of truth, justice, beauty, sublimity, and the grandeur and universality of nature, ought to convince the ever doubting mind that we have a higher than a merely animal-intellectual nature, for these powers do not exist for the animal, nor for "orthodox science"; they belong to man's spiritual nature, and their possession furnishes logical evidence of the qualities of his spirit, for if these powers were not in him, his soul could not be impressed with their presence in external nature, for *each principle can recognize only itself.*

The daisies upon the field or the animals in the forest are neither the light nor the life itself, but living forms in which certain qualities of life and light have become manifest. Likewise there is one universal consciousness, which is the root and fountain of every individual consciousness. The forms of men and women are vehicles for the manifestation of consciousness; but not in everyone is this consciousness characterized as that self-recognition of truth which constitutes divine wisdom. Surely the sun is not affected by the qualities of the products caused by the manifestations of its light in terrestrial forms; he would exist all the same, even if there were no such products; but the forms themselves need the presence of the sun and his light, if they are to live and exist. Thus there is no reason why the divine principle in man should concern itself with the affairs of the terrestrial personality, in which it strives to manifest its own qualities; while it is of the highest importance for these individual minds that they should cling to the light of truth in them, for that which is not true in them is false, and illusive and cannot enter into the true life. God without man is nothing to man, because a man without God is nothing to God. A man without any recognition of that which alone is real in him, is a mere apparition without any reality; his recognition of the power of God, the truth, the real in man, is all that can really be called his own.

Motion and life are universal in nature; but the belief in this fact would serve me very little if my own form were paralyzed and without life. Not the life of another, but the life manifested in me is my own. Thus it is with the worship of God. The belief in a universal God external to myself will serve me little if by my own self-conceit I prevent the manifestation of God in myself. The power of another person is not our own. Only that which grows into power in us is truly *our* power. Like the sleeping princess in the enchanted castle the spark of the self-consciousness of God in man sleeps within the human soul until it is awakened by the power of divine love becoming active within his own heart. Then will the soul, the life, of man recognize its own divine nature and immortality, for immortality will recognize itself in the soul. There is no outside power of any kind that can save man, if that power does not become manifested in him. It is therefore not to any outside God or gods, but to the light in ourselves that we must look for redemption from darkness. This light of divine wisdom is neither the visible light in nature, nor the deceptive light of the arguing intellect, but the spiritual light of divine wisdom becoming manifest in the soul produces the interior awakening from an illusive existence into real life in divine truth.

What then must we do for the purpose of attaining divine wisdom ? The answer to this question is plain: We must let divine wisdom become manifested in us by ceasing to cling to that which will hinder its manifestation. We cannot expect to be redeemed from ignorance by that conception of self which is itself the product of our own ignorance; we cannot by the exercise of the will of our illusive self transform ourselves into gods, this will being itself an illusion, nor by fancying ourselves, to be gods become gods in reality; all that we can really do, is, by the power which we have already received from our own real self, cause "the illusive self to disappear in its nothingness and become inactive, so that the falsehoods will die and the truth in us become manifest. Thus we need not trouble our brains and exercise our ingenuity for the purpose of finding out what we shall do to save that "self", which is an illusion and which cannot be saved, it having never had any real and permanent life of its own, but being like a cloud in the sky, that changes its form and disappears; while our real self is already safe and only awaits our recognition of its own divine state.

We find it stated in many books that we must sacrifice our self-will to God; and this has been unfortunately misinterpreted by many that there should be no will, and that one must abandon himself to the power of unknown influences such as may choose to take possession of him. Such a misunderstanding is detrimental in the highest degree, and would make us helpless instruments in the hands of the powers of darkness. The divine will is the greatest of all powers in the possession of man, and "to sacrifice the self-will to God" does not mean to sacrifice it to nothing. It means to cease to leave the power of will at the disposal of the falsehoods constituting the illusive self, and to employ it in the service of the power of truth. Thus by bringing the will with which we are endowed into harmony with the will of God, our power to will does not become extinct nor annihilated, but is lifted up higher and becomes itself divine and free from the domination of the illusive self. The divine will is divine love, and the love of God is the love of truth, the recognition of light, which destroys the love for the illusive self and its self-interests and selfish desires, which are the products of egotism and non-recognition of truth. There can be no annihilation of self-will by means of the self-will. The illusion of "self" must itself disappear, and when this misconception has once been dissolved in the light of divine wisdom, then will its will and desires have also ceased to exist.

This love to God is not a sentimental attraction towards something objective, external, unknown, or imaginary; it is the self-recognition of the power of love, by itself and in everything, which can take place only after love (the will) has become free from the delusion of the so-called self.

The "I" is the great delusion which captures the mind, whether we refer it to the limited "lower self" or to come "higher self", which we limit in our imagination. The idea of self presupposes the existence of another. If I imagine that besides my true self, the truth, there is still another truth, I am then not realizing the one and the all. If I delude myself in believing that I am the segment of a circle, existing at its periphery, I do not realize ray true universal nature. I can recognize my true nature as all in all only if I reside at the centre, from which I can perceive in every direction the all of my nature, wherein no sense of limitation and separation exists.

This disappearance of the one in the one, the limited in the infinite; this giving up of the illusion of limitation in the universal divine self-consciousness of the truth, is the meaning of the often-used and rarely-understood expression, "to die in the Christ"; and there is no other way of attaining this glorious resurrection except by the death of that which is illusive and false. There is nothing in man that can have any real knowledge of God, except God in him. *To really know is to be.* It is not that "Mr. Smith" or "Mrs. Brown" can truly know God; but if God recognizes His own true self in them, then will divine wisdom in them arise and become manifest, and there will be no more "Mr. Smith" or "Mrs. Brown", they are only external forms in which this manifestation takes place.

This self-recognition of the one and eternal truth in man is also testified to by *Gautama Buddha*; for after having attained his interior illumination, he did not state that by his own personal cleverness he had obtained real knowledge of the causes of sorrow; but he said, "This noble truth concerning the origin of sorrow was not, O Bikkhus, among the doctrines handed down; but *there arose within me the eye* (the power to perceive it); *there arose the understanding; there arose the wisdom; there arose the light*" (Dhamma-Kakka-Tattavatana-Sutta).

Unsanctified man cannot sanctify himself; he can only desist from clinging to that which is an obstacle to his becoming sanctified by the power of divine grace, or the light acting in him. This power of divine grace, which is in ourselves and everywhere, is the only means for salvation — not for the salvation of that illusion of "I," which constitutes at present our personal identity, and which cannot be saved — but for that salvation which takes place if man recognizes his own true divine nature, and thus becomes himself the reality.

Thus real "*practical occultism*" does not consist in the selfish acquisition of certain secrets of nature which may be used for the benefit of the personal self, but in *the art to die* to the darkness; so that the divine life and light may become manifest. It means that while the true lover of wisdom lives, still it is not he who truly lives, but the truth (the Christ) is living and manifested in him. This cannot be accomplished by the illusion of self, for ignorance cannot will ignorance, self cannot destroy self; but it may be accomplished by the practice of *Yoga*, which means the habitual recognition of the power of divine truth in oneself. The illusive self is an illusion, and therefore all of its apparent knowledge of truth, all of its virtues and vices are equally merely appearances. If we know divine wisdom in us, we need no other knowledge; if the truth recognizes itself in us, there will be an end to desire. All that can possibly be good or virtuous in a man is the manifestation of goodness and virtue in him.

It is surely an absurdity to offer selfish petitions to some external god, and, speaking from the personal point of view, to say, "O Lord, give *me* this or that!" Such a "prayer" is a manifestation of selfishness, and identical with asserting that we pretend to be something besides God, and that God is not the all in all. We should not ask anything for the benefit of what is false in ourselves, but let the falsehoods die in the light of the truth, so that the truth itself may become manifest.

Let then the "student of Occultism" cease to run after chimeras and fancies, and seek by becoming true to realize the nature of divine truth. Let him seek to facilitate the manifestation of truth in him, and increase its power by acting according to truth and doing his duty on all planes of existence. Let him not fear to act wrongly if he acts according to the dictates of the truth in him. He who acts according to his inmost conviction of truth is a saint; he who lives in fear is a fool. The highest wisdom is obedience to divine law, and from the death of egotism arises the true realization of the highest ideal, the self-knowledge of divine wisdom in man.

ORACLES

(Translated by Thomas Taylor.)

DIVINITY is never so much turned away from man, and never so much sends him novel paths, as when we make our ascent to the most divine of speculations, or works, in a confused or disordered manner, and as it adds, with unhallowed lips, or unbathed feet. For of those, who are thus negligent, the progressions are imperfect, the impulses are vain, and the paths are blind.

PROCL. IN PARMENID.

-oOo-

THINGS divine cannot be obtained by those whose intellectual eye is directed to body; but those only can arrive at possession of them, who, stript of their garments, hasten to the summit.

PROCL. IN CRAT.

-oOo-

THE oracles often give the victory to our own choice, and not the order alone of the mundane periods. As for instance, when they say, "On beholding yourself fear." And again, "Believe yourself above body, and you are." And still further, when they assert, "That our sorrows germinate in us voluntarily as the growth of the particular life which we lead."

www.ingramcontent.com/pod-product-compliance
Lightning Source LLC
LaVergne TN
LVHW041503070426
835507LV00009B/785